TRANSFO

MW01610376

A Study of...

the Fruit of the Spirit
Love, Joy, and Peace
versus
the Work of the Flesh
Self-Love, Frustration, and Worry

By:
Steven Curington

Book 2—Transformer Workbook
Copyright © 2004
Steven Curington & Reformers Unanimous
Published by Boyd Stevens Publishers
Rockford, IL 61132
Printed in Canada.

Congratulations on your recent completion of the Reformers Unanimous *Challenger* Workbook. You have read the Bible, studied the Bible, memorized the Bible, and heard the Bible (preached). These forms of learning will be continued throughout this course.

Now that you have made it this far in the program, you are beginning to experience some success in your new Christian life. Remember that new levels bring new devils. Be careful. As you are developing spiritually, please remember the importance of not only learning *about* God, but getting to *know* God. You will grow in your knowledge of God as you learn to yield to His leading.

You will now begin Book 2—*Transformer* Workbook. Books 2, 3, and 4 are patterned after the fruit of the Spirit as outlined in Galatians 5:22-25—*But the fruit of the Spirit is **love, joy, peace, longsuffering, gentleness, goodness, faith, meekness, temperance**: against such there is no law. And they that are Christ's have crucified the flesh with the affections and lusts. If we live in the Spirit, let us also walk in the Spirit.*

Fruit means "outcome, or result." The outcome or result of planting an apple seed in the ground is apples. Though this process takes time (patience), with the proper watering (application of the Holy Spirit) and care (time spent in prayer) and labor (time spent in study), you will receive the desired outcome or result. With this amazing truth in mind, what would be the fruit of the Spirit? Well, of course, it would be the outcome or result of the Spirit of God leading you.

In this book, you will be introduced to the *It's Personal* Daily Journal. Your relationship with the Lord is of the utmost importance to your recovery process. Be sure to effectively use your journal as a means of developing that love relationship with God that He yearns to have with you. If you do, you will find the freedom that can make you free... *finally*.

Serving the One who died for all,

Steven Curington
President

FRUIT OF THE SPIRIT~LOVE
vs.
WORK OF THE FLESH~SELF-LOVE

CHALLENGE 1

Memorize the biblical definition of Love

Love is *the willing, sacrificial giving of oneself for the benefit of others without thought of return.*

Meaning: Whenever God leads you to respond to someone's need by expressing love, you will try to help that person in a way that primarily benefits them. You will do this by giving of yourself in a sacrificial way. This is God working through you. Whenever you allow this to happen you are under the influence of the Spirit of God and it will lead to great joy.

To complete this challenge, you must memorize the biblical definition of love.

Challenge Complete _____ Date _____
                                        (Student Signature)

Challenge Complete _____ Date _____
                                        (Leader Signature)

CHALLENGE 2

Memorize the definition of Self-Love

Self-love is *the willing or unwilling giving of oneself to others with selfish thoughts of return.*

Meaning: Unlike the leading of the Spirit that will cause us to give unselfishly, the outside influence of the devil will lead us to give only when it provides a benefit in return to us.   This is the difference between when God is leading us and when we are leading ourselves. Are you responding to the needs of others under the influence of the Spirit in love, or do you focus on what will personally benefit you?

To complete this challenge, you must memorize the definition of self-love.

Challenge Complete _____ Date _____
(Student Signature)

Challenge Complete _____ Date _____
(Leader Signature)

CHALLENGE 3

Review Love vs. Self-love

Having memorized the definitions of love and self-love, take the time to consider each meaning and meditate or think upon them.   In conclusion, write a brief explanation of how these truths will help you to avoid walking after the flesh but rather walk in the Spirit.

_____

_____

_____

_____

_____

_____

_____

_____

_____

Challenge Complete _____ Date _____
                              (Student Signature)

Challenge Complete _____ Date _____
                              (Leader Signature)

CHALLENGE 4

Memorize Matthew 22:37-40

Jesus said unto him, Thou shalt love the Lord thy God with all thy heart, and with all thy soul, and with all thy mind. This is the first and great commandment. And the second is like unto it, Thou shalt love thy neighbour as thyself. On these two commandments hang all the law and the prophets.   Matthew 22:37-40

What did Jesus mean when He said, *On these two commandments hang all the law and the prophets*? If you are unsure, please re-read chapter 2 of the RU textbook, *Nevertheless I Live*.

_____

_____

_____

_____

Do you believe the above verses prove that God intends to lead you to give sacrificially of yourself for the benefit of others?   Yes or No   (circle one)

Special Note: When we love God or our neighbor under the condition that we receive something in return, then we are not yielding to God's unselfish love. You are yielding to your own selfish love. God's love causes us to enjoy the abundant Christian life. Selfish love leads to the redundant Christian life.

Challenge Complete _____ Date _____
                              (Student Signature)

Challenge Complete _____ Date _____
                              (Leader Signature)

CHALLENGE 5

Essay Report on Matthew 5:1-12

The Bible uses the term, "blessed," which means happy. The formula for exhibiting undeserved happiness is found in Matthew 5:1-12. To complete this challenge, you must read Matthew 5:1-12 and, on a separate sheet of paper, write a 50-or-more-word essay on what you believe Matthew 5:1-12 means to a believer. We encourage you to use any study material necessary to complete your report. We suggest a concordance and King James Version Study Bible. If you would like to borrow some materials for this challenge, you may request them from your counsel leader.

Before you begin, pray that God will give you wisdom in discerning the meaning of this chapter. You should conclude your essay with an explanation of how you can apply this chapter to your life.

Do you believe that by yielding to God's leading to express the characteristics of the Beatitudes that you will find yourself expressing the fruit of the Spirit~Love more often?   Yes or No   (circle one)

Special Note: When God's love is flowing from us in an unselfish and giving way, it will lead us toward some of the happiest times in our life. We will truly know what it means to be "blessed."

Challenge Complete _____ Date _____
                                        (Student Signature)

Challenge Complete _____ Date _____
                                        (Leader Signature)

CHALLENGE 6

Nevertheless I Live Requirement

To complete this challenge, you must listen to Chapter 2—"The Two Commandments of Christ" of the *Nevertheless I Live* tape series, or read Chapter 2 of the *Nevertheless I Live* textbook. If you do not have either of these, please ask your counsel leader to assist you in getting them.

Please explain what chapter 2 teaches us about God's commandments:

1. Christ's teaching on loving God:

_____

_____

2. Christ's teaching on loving others:

_____

_____

Challenge Complete _____ Date _____

(Student Signature)

Challenge Complete _____ Date _____

(Leader Signature)

CHALLENGE 7

Attendance Requirement

To complete this challenge, you must attend a local church **2 Sunday School classes** in your local church. The church you attend must comply with the standards that God has outlined in the Bible. He requests that we worship at a Bible-believing, Bible-teaching church that preaches salvation through grace and not by works. Baptism is taught as a sign of obedience and not a requirement for heaven. They must believe the Bible is the Word of God and is without error, preserved as such for the believer.

Church Attended _____ Date _____

Sunday School Class Attended _____ Date _____

Teacher's Signature _____

Challenge Complete _____ Date _____
(Student Signature)

Challenge Complete _____ Date _____
(Leader Signature)

CHALLENGE 8

It's Personal **Daily Journal**

Challenges are a lot of hard work and bring with them
many great rewards. This is because God has always
wanted to communicate with you the way that you are
now communicating with Him. You see, God will
communicate with you in one of five ways:
1. Through Bible Reading
2. Through Prayer
3. Through Preaching and Teaching
4. Through Christian Friends
5. Through the Holy Spirit

To complete this challenge, you must complete 10 days
of the *It's Personal* Daily Journal. They do not have to
be 10 days in a row and you can continue in your
workbook while you are logging your 10 days of daily
communication with God. You also do not need to
utilize all five forms of communication every day,
though the more forms you use, the closer you will grow
to our Lord.

The *It's Personal* Daily Journal can be purchased through your Reformers book table. In the front of the journal is a detailed explanation of how it works and why it works so well in enhancing your personal relationship with God.

Challenge Complete _____ Date _____
(Student Signature)

Challenge Complete _____ Date _____
(Leader Signature)

CHALLENGE 9

300 Club—Participation Club

To complete this challenge, you must score at least 75 points in **one** seven-day period. If you will do this four times in one month, you will earn membership in the RU 300 Club. On the next page is a score chart that you can fill in to help you keep track of your points for the week.

This is an important club. It shows your willingness to engage in every aspect of the RU program. Remember, if you want to experience the Spirit's leading, you must participate when the Spirit is feeding.

If you attend an RU discipleship class, please write your score on your challenge group score card and give it to your group helper so your score will be added toward earning 300 points for the month. Though this challenge only requires that you score 75 points for one week, I encourage you to earn this total every week for at least one month. If you will score 300 points per month, you will be surprised how fast you will grow spiritually.

Church Service Attendance (10 points for each)	
Sunday School	_____
Sunday Morning	_____
Sunday Evening	_____
Mid Week	_____
RU Class	_____
Total points for Attendance:	_____

Daily Journaling (4 points for each day)	
Sunday	_____
Monday	_____
Tuesday	_____
Wednesday	_____
Thursday	_____
Friday	_____
Saturday	_____
Total points for Journaling:	_____

300 Club

Miscellaneous Points	
Challenges completed for the week (4 points each)	_____
Wearing an RU uniform and/or awards (5 points)	_____
Distributing 7 RU brochures in a week (5 points), or	_____
Placing a poster in a place of business (5 points), or	_____
Attending a church-sponsored outreach (5 points)	_____
Total Miscellaneous Points:	_____

TOTAL WEEKLY POINTS			
Service Total:	Journaling Total:	Miscellaneous Total:	WEEK'S TOTAL:
_____	_____	_____	_____

Challenge Complete _____ Date _____
(Student Signature)

Challenge Complete _____ Date _____
(Leader Signature)

CHALLENGE 10

Memorize I Corinthians 13:1-2

Though I speak with the tongues of men and of angels, and have not charity (love), I am become as sounding brass, or a tinkling cymbal.   I Corinthians 13:1

Challenge Complete _____ Date _____
(Leader Signature)

And though I have the gift of prophecy, and understand all mysteries, and all knowledge; and though I have all faith, so that I could remove mountains, and have not charity (love), *I am nothing.*   I Corinthians 13:2

Please describe in your own words what these verses mean to you.

_____

_____

_____

Do you believe that by accepting the verses listed above you can better yield to the fruit of the Spirit~Love?
Yes or No
(circle one)

Special Note: No matter how much talent you have, if you have selfish love toward others, you are wasting your time helping others. You may be helping them, but you are not helping yourself. Selfish love is of the flesh. Unselfish love is of the Spirit. When we do things in our flesh, we are not pleasing God.

Challenge Complete _____ Date _____
(Student Signature)

Challenge Complete _____ Date _____
(Leader Signature)

CHALLENGE 11

Essay Report on Matthew 5:41-47

Earlier in this workbook, you began a study in Matthew chapter 5. Please read the remaining verses in Matthew 5 and write an essay of 50 words or more on what you believe Matthew 5:41-47 (an example of Christian love demonstrated) means to a believer. If you would like to borrow some materials for this challenge, you may request them from your counsel leader.

Pray that God would give you wisdom in discerning the meaning of these verses. You should conclude your essay with an explanation of how you can apply these verses to your life.

Do you believe these verses can help you exhibit the fruit of the Spirit~Love?   Yes or No   (circle one)

Challenge Complete _____ Date _____
(Student Signature)

Challenge Complete _____ Date _____
(Leader Signature)

CHALLENGE 12

Attendance Requirement

To complete this challenge, you must attend a local church **Sunday morning** service in your community. The church you attend must comply with the standards that God has outlined in the Bible. He requests that we worship at a Bible-believing, Bible-teaching church that preaches salvation through grace and not by works. Baptism is taught as a sign of obedience and not a requirement for heaven. They must believe the Bible is the Word of God and is without error, preserved as such for the believer.

Church Attended _____ Date _____

Topic of Sermon _____

Challenge Complete _____ Date _____
(Pastor's signature– signifying agreement with standards listed above)

Challenge Complete _____ Date _____
(Student Signature)

Challenge Complete _____ Date _____
(Leader Signature)

CHALLENGE 13

Word Study on the First Commandment
(Found in Matthew 22:36-38)

In Challenge 4, you memorized Matthew 22:37-40. To complete this challenge, you must do a word study on these verses. You may use a dictionary to find the word meanings. You will also find the definitions in the *Nevertheless I Live* Chapter 2.

Define "Heart" _____

_____

Define "Soul" _____

_____

Define "Mind" _____

_____

Define "All" _____

_____

Using the previous definition of love, as well as the definitions above, please dissect and define Matthew 22:37 and rewrite it in your own words:

_____

_____

_____

_____

_____

Do you believe that by accepting this verse you can better yield to the fruit of the Spirit~Love?   Yes or No
(circle one)

Challenge Complete _____ Date _____
                        (Student Signature)

Challenge Complete _____ Date _____
                        (Leader Signature)

CHALLENGE 14

Memorize I Corinthians 13:3-4

And though I bestow all my goods to feed the poor, and though I give my body to be burned, and have not charity, it profiteth me nothing.   1 Corinthians 13:3

Challenge Complete _____ Date _____
                              (Student Signature)

Charity suffereth long, and is kind; charity envieth not; charity vaunteth not itself, is not puffed up,
                                        1 Corinthians 13:4

Please describe in your own words what these verses mean to you.

_____

_____

_____

_____

Do you believe that by accepting these verses you can better yield to the fruit of the Spirit~Love?   Yes or No
                                              (circle one)

Special Note: Once again, if you give with selfish motives (no matter how great your sacrifice), it is a waste of your time. These verses tell us that it profits us nothing!

Challenge Complete _____ Date _____
                              (Student Signature)

Challenge Complete _____ Date _____
                              (Leader Signature)

CHALLENGE 15

Service Opportunity

To complete this challenge, you must perform an act of love, expecting nothing in return. If you think about it, you may realize that you have done so since the beginning of this study on love. It does not have to be anything large or obvious. It just needs to be a sacrificial gift of yourself without thought of your own personal benefit.

Act of love shown to another _____

_____

_____

Challenge Complete _____ Date _____
                          (Student Signature)

Challenge Complete _____ Date _____
                          (Leader Signature)

CHALLENGE 16

Word Study on the Second Commandment
(Found in Matthew 22:39) (Read Luke 10:29-37)

In Challenge 4, you memorized Matthew 22:37-40. To complete this challenge, you must **read Luke 10:29-37** and do a word study on Matthew 22:39. You may use a dictionary to find the word meanings. You will also find the definitions in the *Nevertheless I Live* Textbook, chapter two.

Define "Neighbor" _____

_____

Define "Thyself" _____

_____

Using the previous definition of love, as well as the definitions above, please dissect and define Matthew 22:39 and rewrite it in your own words:

_____

_____

_____

_____

Do you believe this verse can help you yield to the fruit of the Spirit~Love?   Yes or No   (circle one)

Challenge Complete _____ Date _____
                              (Student Signature)

Challenge Complete _____ Date _____
                              (Leader Signature)

CHALLENGE 17

Verse Comparison Study

To complete this challenge, you must study the following verses that show the ultimate demonstration of love:

Bible Passage	**Act of Love**
John 3:16	_____
1 John 4:10-11	_____
Matthew 26-27	_____
Ephesians 5:2	_____
1 John 3:16-17	_____
Romans 5:8	_____

After completing this comparison study, please describe in your own words what John 15:12-13 means to you.

This is my commandment, That ye love one another, as I have loved you. Greater love hath no man than this, that a man lay down his life for his friends.

John 15:12-13

How do these verses show us how we ought to love others?

_____

_____

_____

_____

Special Note: No one has ever loved the way Jesus loved us. I John 4:19 tells us that God loved us before we even loved Him. When you became His child, He placed His Spirit within you. Now, the love of Christ dwells within us. We may not be required to die for others, but we can live for others. We show God's love to others by yielding to the fruit of the Spirit~Love.

Challenge Complete _____ Date _____
                          (Student Signature)

Challenge Complete _____ Date _____
                          (Leader Signature)

CHALLENGE 18

Memorize I Corinthians 13:5-8a

[Charity (or, love)] *Doth not behave itself unseemly, seeketh not her own, is not easily provoked, thinketh no evil;*   I Corinthians 13:5

Challenge Complete _____ Date _____
                          (Helper Signature)

Rejoiceth not in iniquity, but rejoiceth in the truth;
                                        I Corinthians 13:6

Challenge Complete _____ Date _____
                          (Helper Signature)

Beareth all things, believeth all things, hopeth all things, endureth all things. Charity never faileth...
                                        1 Corinthians 13:7-8a

Please describe in your own words what these verses mean to you.

_____

_____

_____

Do you believe that by accepting these verses you can better yield to the fruit of the Spirit~Love?   Yes or No
(circle one)

Challenge Complete _____ Date _____
(Student Signature)

Challenge Complete _____ Date _____
(Leader Signature)

Congratulations! You have completed your study on the fruit of the Spirit~Love and the work of the flesh~Self-Love. You have learned more of the ultimate sacrifice of love, God's gift of His Son for our sins. You have read, studied, and memorized verses that demonstrate the power and importance of love. It truly can change your life. The real test of whether or not you are yielding to this fruit of love is found in your actions and reactions toward the needy that God may place in your life. When faced with these types of opportunities, take the time to consider how Jesus would have you respond. Surely, if He leads you to respond, then you would sacrificially give of yourself for the benefit of that person, without selfish thoughts of return. That is the fruit of the Spirit~Love. If you are a child of God, then this love lies within you. However, the goal of the devil, your adversary, is to get you to settle for the work of the flesh~Self-Love. Reject all your selfish desires to receive something in return for your sacrificial giving and your relationship with God and others will grow.

Next, we will study the fruit of the Spirit~Joy. Ask the Lord to help you stay committed to this path which will lead to the spirtual growth necessary to remain free from all strongholds... *finally*.

FRUIT OF THE SPIRIT~JOY
vs.
WORK OF THE FLESH~FRUSTRATION

CHALLENGE 1

Memorize the biblical definition of Joy

Joy is *a cheerful, calm delight and rejoicing in a particular circumstance.*

Meaning: When we are faced with circumstances in life that are less than enjoyable, our natural tendency is to think the worst. However, under the influence of the Spirit, we realize that God intends these circumstances to be for our good. As a result of this realization, our proper response from God will be to remain calm and delight in our "less-than-enjoyable" circumstances.

To complete this challenge, you must memorize the biblical definition of joy.

Challenge Complete _____ Date _____
                              (Student Signature)

Challenge Complete _____ Date _____
                              (Leader Signature)

CHALLENGE 2

Memorize the definition of Frustration

Frustration *is a rejection or unhappy refusal in the circumstances of life.*

Meaning: Unlike the leading of the Spirit, which will cause us to express joy when life's circumstances seem bad, the outside influence of the enemy will lead us to express unhappiness toward or reject these same circumstances.   When you yield to one over the other, it determines whether God is leading you or whether you are leading yourself.   As you grow in the Lord, it is important that you monitor your "joy meter."   Are you able to handle more of your difficult circumstances under the influence of joy?   Or, do you find yourself frustrated regularly at every little thing that goes wrong?   If so, then you are yielding to the work of the flesh~Frustration.   However, only you can choose your response to the circumstances of life.   Choose to exhibit joy in your life's circumstances!   Then leave it in God's hands to work it all out.

To complete this challenge, you must memorize the definition of frustration.

Challenge Complete _____ Date _____
                              (Student Signature)

Challenge Complete _____ Date _____
                              (Leader Signature)

CHALLENGE 3

Review Joy vs. Frustration

Having memorized the definitions of joy and frustration, take the time to consider each meaning and meditate or think upon them.   In conclusion, write a brief explanation of how these truths will help you to avoid walking after the flesh, but rather walk in the Spirit.

_____

_____

_____

_____

Challenge Complete _____ Date _____
(Student Signature)

Challenge Complete _____ Date _____
(Leader Signature)

CHALLENGE 4

Attendance Requirement

To complete this challenge, you must attend a local church **Sunday morning** service in your community. The church you attend must comply with the standards that God has outlined in the Bible. He requests that we worship at a Bible-believing, Bible-teaching church that preaches salvation through grace and not by works. Baptism is taught as a sign of obedience and not a requirement for heaven. They must believe the Bible is the Word of God and is without error, preserved as such for the believer.

Church Attended _____ Date _____

Topic of Sermon _____

Challenge Complete _____ Date _____
(Pastor's signature– signifying agreement with standards listed above)

Challenge Complete _____ Date _____
(Student Signature)

Challenge Complete _____ Date _____
(Leader Signature)

CHALLENGE 5

10/40 Window of Opportunity

To complete this challenge, you must choose and complete one "Window of Opportunity" of which are listed below. Materials listed in Windows 1 and 2 will be provided for you at no charge from your RU director.

1. **Window of Opportunity One:** Place *10 RU posters* in businesses or workplaces within *40 days*.
   - You must provide a complete list of participating businesses or workplaces, including contact name and phone number for each.

2. **Window of Opportunity Two:** Distribute *10 RU brochures* or *church brochures* for *40 days*.

3. **Window of Opportunity Three:** Invite a visitor that will attend at least *10 church and RU services* over the course of *40 days*.
   - You may bring anyone that you think could use the lessons that you are learning in class, especially someone that you believe may be unsaved.

4. **Window of Opportunity Four:** Win *10 unsaved people to Christ* in *40 days*.
   - Each name and address should be turned in to your RU director for proper follow up.

We consider this to be the most prestigious award in Reformers Unanimous because it shows that you are sharing your faith. That is what Jesus commanded us to do until He returns. There is great reward in heaven for sharing your faith, therefore we believe there ought to be great reward here on earth from those in leadership training you. We hop you will try to complete as many of these *Windows of Opportunity* as possible. You will be required to complete this challenge in each of the remaining two workbooks—the *Conformer* and *Reformer*.

Upon successful completion of a *Window of Opportunity*, you will receive a 10/40 Window badge at your next RU awards ceremony.

Window of Opportunity Completed: _____

Challenge Complete _____ Date _____
                         (Student Signature)

Challenge Complete _____ Date _____
                         (Leader Signature)

CHALLENGE 6

Memorize Psalms 51:12-13

Restore unto me the joy of thy salvation; and uphold me with thy free spirit. Then will I teach transgressors thy ways; and sinners shall be converted unto thee.

Psalms 51:12-13

What takes place when your joy is restored?

_____

_____

How ought we respond to the restoration process?

_____

_____

Do you believe the above request can help you yield to the fruit of the Spirit~Joy?   Yes or No   (circle one)

Special Note: When you got saved, God gave you the fruit of joy.   However, in our search for temporal happiness in life, we often find ourselves frustrated. This does not lend itself to the abundant Christian life, but rather the redundant Christian life. If you are guilty of searching for happiness rather than being content with God's joy, and your search has led you to unnecessary frustration, please ask the Lord to restore you back into fellowship with Him. He will restore unto you the joy of your salvation.

Challenge Complete _____ Date _____
                                          (Student Signature)

Challenge Complete _____ Date _____
                                          (Leader Signature)

CHALLENGE 7

Reading Lesson: Philippians 1-4

To complete this challenge, you must read Philippians 1-4. Below are spaces to list the topics of each chapter.

Please fill these blanks in after you have completed each chapter.

Chapter 1 _____

Chapter 2 _____

Chapter 3 _____

Chapter 4 _____

Please describe how the above chapters can be applied in your efforts to yield to the fruit of the Spirit~Joy.

_____

_____

_____

Challenge Complete _____ Date _____
                              (Student Signature)

Challenge Complete _____ Date _____
                              (Leader Signature)

CHALLENGE 8

New Testament Books of the Bible

Matthew   *Acts*
Mark   *Romans*
Luke   *I Corinthians*
John   *II Corinthians*

To complete this challenge, you must memorize the first 8 books of the New Testament in order. This will help you in finding passages quickly and will enhance your knowledge of God's Holy Word.

Challenge Complete _____ Date _____
(Student Signature)

Challenge Complete _____ Date _____
(Leader Signature)

CHALLENGE 9

Attendance Requirement

To complete this challenge, you must attend a local church **Sunday evening** service in your community. The church you attend must comply with the standards that God has outlined in the Bible. He requests that we worship at a Bible-believing, Bible-teaching church that preaches salvation through grace and not by works. Baptism is taught as a sign of obedience and not a requirement for heaven. They must believe the Bible is the Word of God and is without error, preserved as such for the believer.

Church Attended _____ Date _____

Topic of Sermon _____

Challenge Complete _____ Date _____
(Pastor's signature– signifying agreement with standards listed above)

Challenge Complete _____ Date _____
(Student Signature)

Challenge Complete _____ Date _____
(Leader Signature)

CHALLENGE 10

Memorize Psalm 126:5-6

They that sow in tears shall reap in joy. He that goeth forth and weepeth, bearing precious seed, shall doubtless come again with rejoicing, bringing his sheaves with him.   Psalm 126:5-6

What will you reap if you will put forth an effort (one that affects your emotions) in doing the Lord's work?

_____

_____

_____

_____

Special Note: If we will go and tell others about Christ with great concern for their souls, God says we will return with fruit that remains. That fruit will cause you to rejoice (i.e., "repeatable joy"). It is always worthwhile to do God's work God's way. Whenever we try to do God's work our way, we always end up frustrated.

Do you believe these verses can help you yield to the fruit of the Spirit~Joy?   Yes or No   (circle one)

Challenge Complete _____ Date _____
                         (Student Signature)

Challenge Complete _____ Date _____
                         (Leader Signature)

CHALLENGE 11

Reading Lesson: Luke 1-4 (Tidings of great Joy)

To complete this challenge, you must read Luke 1-4. Below are spaces to list the topics of each chapter. Please fill in these blanks after you have completed each chapter.

Chapter 1 _____

Chapter 2 _____

Chapter 3 _____

Chapter 4 _____

Please describe how the above chapters can be applied in your efforts to yield to the fruit of the Spirit~Joy.

_____

_____

_____

_____

_____

Challenge Complete _____ Date _____
(Student Signature)

Challenge Complete _____ Date _____
(Leader Signature)

CHALLENGE 12

New Testament Books of the Bible

Galatians   *I Thessalonians*
Ephesians   *II Thessalonians*
Phillipians   *I Timothy*
Colossians   *II Timothy*

To complete this challenge, you must memorize the second 8 books of the New Testament in order. This will help you in finding passages quickly and will enhance your knowledge of God's Holy Word.

Challenge Complete _____ Date _____
                      (Student Signature)

Challenge Complete _____ Date _____
                      (Leader Signature)

CHALLENGE 13

Nevertheless I Live Requirement

To complete this challenge, you must listen to Chapter 3—"Three Dedications for Discerning God's Direction" of the *Nevertheless I Live* tape series, or read Chapter 3 of the *Nevertheless I Live* textbook. If you do not have either of these, please ask your counsel leader to assist you in getting them.

Please explain what chapter 3 teaches us about knowing and doing God's will for your life.

1. Step one for knowing God's will is...

_____

_____

2. Step two for knowing God's will is...

_____

_____

3. Step three for knowing God's will is...

_____

_____

Challenge Complete _____ Date _____
                              (Student Signature)

Challenge Complete _____ Date _____
                              (Leader Signature)

CHALLENGE 14

300 Club—Participation Club

To complete this challenge, you must score at least 75 points in **one** seven-day period. If you will do this four times in one month, you will earn membership in the RU 300 Club.

If you attend an RU discipleship class, please write your score on your challenge group score card and give it to your group helper so your score will be added toward earning 300 points for the month. Though this challenge only requires that you score 75 points for one week, I encourage you to earn this total every week for at least one month. If you will score 300 points per month, you will be surprised how fast you will grow spiritually.

Challenge Complete _____ Date _____
(Student Signature)

Challenge Complete _____ Date _____
(Leader Signature)

Church Service Attendance **(10 points for each)**

Sunday School   _____

Sunday Morning   _____

Sunday Evening   _____

Mid Week   _____

RU Class   _____

Total points for Attendance: _____

300 Club

Daily Journaling **(4 points for each day)**

Sunday   _____

Monday   _____

Tuesday   _____

Wednesday   _____

Thursday   _____

Friday   _____

Saturday   _____

Total points for Journaling: _____

Miscellaneous Points	
Challenges completed for the week (4 points each)	_____
Wearing an RU uniform and/or awards (5 points)	_____
Distributing 7 RU brochures in a week (5 points), or	_____
Placing a poster in a place of business (5 points), or	_____
Attending a church-sponsored outreach (5 points)	_____
Total Miscellaneous Points:	_____

TOTAL WEEKLY POINTS			
Service Total:	**Journaling Total:**	**Miscellaneous Total:**	**WEEK'S TOTAL:**
_____	_____	_____	_____

CHALLENGE 15

It's Personal **Daily Journal**

To complete this challenge, you must complete 10 days of the *It's Personal* Daily Journal. They do not have to be 10 days in a row and you can continue in your workbook while you are logging your 10 days of daily communication with God. You also do not need to utilize all five forms of communication every day, though the more forms you use, the closer you will grow to our Lord.

Challenge Complete _____ Date _____
(Student Signature)

Challenge Complete _____ Date _____
(Leader Signature)

CHALLENGE 16

Memorize Luke 15:10

Likewise, I say unto you, there is joy in the presence of the angels of God over one sinner that repenteth.

Luke 15:10

Please describe in your own words what takes place in heaven when someone changes his mind about his wrong behavior and turns to our Lord for direction in life.

_____

_____

_____

Do you believe this verse can help you yield to the fruit of the Spirit~Joy?   Yes or No   (circle one)

Special Note: Once again we see that one of the results of having a concern for souls is the fruit of joy. You will never know joy until you have experienced the joy of leading someone to Christ. If you have not learned how to do this, maybe you should. Ask your church pastor if training in winning souls to Christ is available in your church. If your church doesn't teach about the value of soul winning, maybe you should look for a different church. As a matter of fact, every church that holds an RU meeting is a soul winning church. Maybe you should attend the church that holds this class. They will help you gain the joy of leading people to the Lord. It might end up to be one of your closest friends or family members that get saved. What a JOY that would be!

Challenge Complete _____ Date _____
(Student Signature)

Challenge Complete _____ Date _____
(Leader Signature)

CHALLENGE 17

Essay Report on "Joy To The World"

The Gospel (Good News) of Jesus Christ can be found in many different forms of communication. Not only is it found in the Bible and in most preaching messages, it may also be found in many spiritual hymns.

To complete this challenge, you must write a 40 word essay on the song "Joy to the World" and give a detailed explanation of what the songwriter was proclaiming as an extreme occassion for joy. If you do not have access to the song, ask your counsel leader to obtain a copy of it for you. Remember to finish your essay with a brief description of how this joy can be realized in your life on a day-to-day basis.

Challenge Complete _____ Date _____
(Student Signature)

Challenge Complete _____ Date _____
(Leader Signature)

CHALLENGE 18

Memorize 3 John 1:4

I have no greater joy than to hear that my children walk in truth.   3 John 1:4

Please describe in your own words what brings God great joy and what that means. If you do not understand it, than re-read chapter 1 of the RU Textbook, *Nevertheless I Live*, part two—the Truth. It will help you understand the lies of society and the Truth—God's Son.

_____

_____

_____

_____

Do you believe this verse can help you yield to the fruit of the Spirit~Joy?   Yes or No   (circle one)

Special Note: We have no reason to be frustrated in our Christian life. In fact, if we appreciate our salvation and accept the benefits of it in its entirety, then we would never prefer to yield to the flesh of frustration.   I encourage you to make a commitment that, no matter the circumstance, you will yield to the fruit of joy. You will enJOY life much more!

Challenge Complete _____ Date _____
                                             (Student Signature)

Challenge Complete _____ Date _____
                                             (Leader Signature)

CHALLENGE 19

Bible Study on Joy

To successfully complete this challenge, you must study the following verses that describe the way that joy is exhibited.

Bible Passage	Act of Joy
Psalm 51:12-13	_____
Psalm 126:5-6	_____
Luke 15:7	_____
Luke 15:10	_____
3 John 1:4	_____

As you may have noticed, joy is received in a person's soul when he focuses his attention on the spiritual condition of others. In your effort to yield to the fruit of the Spirit~Joy, what can you do to increase your focus on the souls of others?

_____

_____

_____

_____

_____

Challenge Complete _____ Date _____
                              (Student Signature)

Challenge Complete _____ Date _____
                              (Leader Signature)

CHALLENGE 20

Reading Lesson: I John

To complete this challenge, you must read the book of 1 John. **1 John 1:4 states that these 5 chapters were written that you may be full of joy.** Below are spaces to list the topics of each chapter. Please fill in these blanks after you have read each chapter.

Chapter 1 _____

Chapter 2 _____

Chapter 3 _____

Chapter 4 _____

Chapter 5 _____

Please describe how the above chapters can be applied to your desire to yield to the fruit of the Spirit~Joy.

_____

_____

_____

_____

_____

Challenge Complete _____ Date _____
                              (Student Signature)

Challenge Complete _____ Date _____
                              (Leader Signature)

Congratulations! You have completed your study on the fruit of the Spirit~Joy. You have read, studied, and memorized many verses that apply to this wonderful expression of God known as JOY. It is available to every believer and is given by the Holy Spirit to those who exercise a concern for lost souls. You see, many of us have spent our lives searching for happiness. Many times we would find it in feeding our sinful appetites. Often, this search for happiness was at the core of our extremely selfish behavior. The problem with searching for happiness is that happiness is temporal. When that happiness is gone, it is replaced with frustration. Joy, on the other hand, lasts forever. A search for joy, rather than happiness, will have at its core an unselfish concern for the needs of others. Oh, you may have bad days. There may be days that you are not happy. However, you will remain content if you have obtained joy. It is such a sweet fruit. Remember to pray that the Lord will help you remain disciplined as you continue your study of the fruit of the Spirit. Your next study will be on the fruit of the Spirit~Peace. You are about to discover a peace that passes all understanding.

FRUIT OF THE SPIRIT~PEACE
vs.
WORK OF THE FLESH~WORRY

CHALLENGE 1

Memorize the biblical definition of Peace

Peace is *to be safe from harm in your spirit, mind, and body*.

Meaning: Peace is the result of a Christian who is expressing love and experiencing joy. Of course, someone who is blessed as such is going to experience great tribulation in his life. You see, God's power will be on the life of that one who expresses love and experiences joy. That power will lead to incredible opportunities for evangelistic outreach, thus bringing oppression from the enemy. To fight this oppression and impending tribulation you must have God's peace that passes all understanding. You will then be free from worry or harm in your spirit, mind, or body.

To complete this challenge you must memorize the biblical definition of peace.

Challenge Complete _____ Date _____
(Student Signature)

Challenge Complete _____ Date _____
(Leader Signature)

CHALLENGE 2

Memorize the definition of Worry

Worry is *to live in fear of harm in your spirit, mind, or body.*

Meaning: Unlike yielding to the Spirit that will cause us to forsake fear, the outside influence of the enemy will cause us to live in fear.   Once again, we see the difference of yielding to the Holy Spirit, or yielding to the outside influence of the devil.   As you grow and develop in your relationship with Christ, measure your "fear factor."   Are you yielding to the peace of God in the circumstances of life, or are you yielding to worry?

Remember, if you are a Christian, you are safe in the protection of your heavenly Father.   Your life's circumstances may seem fearful, but God has it all under control, if you allow Him to control it.   He is able to work *all* things together for your good– even the bad things!   Trust in this truth and let your fears fade away.

To complete this challenge, you must memorize the definition of worry.

Challenge Complete _____ Date _____
(Student Signature)

Challenge Complete _____ Date _____
(Leader Signature)

CHALLENGE 3

Review Peace vs. Worry

Having memorized the definition of peace and worry, take the time to consider each meaning and meditate or think upon them. In conclusion, write a brief explanation of how these truths will help you to avoid walking after the flesh, but rather walk in the Spirit.

_____

_____

_____

_____

_____

_____

Challenge Complete _____ Date _____
(Student Signature)

Challenge Complete _____ Date _____
(Leader Signature)

CHALLENGE 4

Attendance Requirement

To complete this challenge, you must attend a local church **Sunday evening** service in your community. The church you attend must comply with the standards that God has outlined in the Bible. He requests that we worship at a Bible-believing, Bible-teaching church that preaches salvation through grace and not by works. Baptism is taught as a sign of obedience and not a requirement for heaven. They must believe the Bible is the Word of God and is without error, preserved as such for the believer.

Church Attended _____ Date _____

Topic of Sermon _____

Challenge Complete _____ Date _____
(Pastor's signature– signifying agreement with standards listed above)

Challenge Complete _____ Date _____
(Student Signature)

Challenge Complete _____ Date _____
(Leader Signature)

CHALLENGE 5

Memorize Psalm 119:165

Great peace have they which love thy law: and nothing shall offend them.   Psalm 119:165

Please describe in your own words what you will gain if you love God's Word.

_____

_____

_____

Special Note: When you have the right appetite for God's Word, the Bible, you will have peace. Why? Because God's Word makes promises concerning the safety of His children throughout its sacred pages. I encourage you to read more about the promises that God makes to those who are belong to Him. It will help you yield to His peace.

Do you believe this verse can help you yield to the fruit of the Spirit~Peace?   Yes or No   (circle one)

Challenge Complete _____ Date _____
                              (Student Signature)

Challenge Complete _____ Date _____
                              (Leader Signature)

CHALLENGE 6

New Testament Books of the Bible

Titus	*I John*
Philemon	*II John*
Hebrews	*III John*
James	*Jude*
I Peter	*Revelation*
II Peter	

To complete this challenge, you must memorize the last 11 books of the New Testament in order. This will help you in finding passages quickly and will enhance your knowledge of God's Holy Word.

Challenge Complete _____ Date _____
                              (Student Signature)

Challenge Complete _____ Date _____
                              (Leader Signature)

CHALLENGE 7

Reading Lesson: Luke 1-7

To complete this challenge, you must read Luke 1-7. Below are spaces to list the topics of each chapter. Please fill in these blanks after you have read each chapter.

Chapter 1 _____

Chapter 2 _____

Chapter 3 _____

Chapter 4 _____

Chapter 5 _____

Chapter 6 _____

Chapter 7 _____

Please describe how the above chapters can be applied in your efforts to yield to the fruit of the Spirit~Peace.

_____

_____

_____

_____

Challenge Complete _____ Date _____
                         (Student Signature)

Challenge Complete _____ Date _____
                         (Leader Signature)

CHALLENGE 8

Essay Report on "It Is Well"

The Gospel (Good News) of Jesus Christ can be found in many different forms of communication. Not only is it found in the Bible and in most preaching messages, it may also be found in many spiritual hymns.

To complete this challenge, you must write a 40 word essay on the hymn "It Is Well" and give a detailed explanation of what the songwriter was proclaiming as a reason for peace in the midst of trouble. If you do not have access to the song, ask your helper to obtain a copy of it for you. Remember to finish your essay with a brief description on how this Peace can be realized in your life on a day to day basis.

Challenge Complete _____ Date _____
                              (Student Signature)

Challenge Complete _____ Date _____
                              (Leader Signature)

CHALLENGE 9

Memorize Romans 8:6

For to be carnally minded is death; but to be spiritually minded is life and peace.   Romans 8:6

Please describe in your own words what it means to be "spiritually minded."

_____

_____

_____

Do you believe this verse can help you yield to the fruit of the Spirit~Peace?   Yes or No   (circle one)

Special Note: A carnal minded person is one whose mind dwells on what he wants, what he thinks, and what he feels. His mind is controlled by his flesh and will always lead to spiritual death and often a premature physical death. However, a mind that is under the influence of what God wants, what God thinks, and what God feels is thus under the influence of the Spirit. That person is spiritually minded. This leads to a life worth living, full of the peace of God. This is supposed to be the Christian experience, but because we do not allow God to control our minds, unfortunately it is not the experience of most Christians. Yield your mind to God's control and enjoy a life of peace and purpose.

Challenge Complete _____ Date _____
                                    (Student Signature)

Challenge Complete _____ Date _____
                                    (Leader Signature)

CHALLENGE 10

Nevertheless I Live Requirement

To complete this challenge, you must listen to Chapter 4—"The Four R's of Reformers" of the *Nevertheless I Live* tape series, or read Chapter 4 of the *Nevertheless I Live* textbook. If you do not have either of these, please ask your counsel leader to assist you in getting them.

Please explain what chapter 4 teaches about allowing Christ to live His life through you.

1. Explain what is taught on reaffirming our helplessness:

_____

_____

_____

2. Explain what is taught on realizing our new identity in Christ:

_____

_____

_____

3. Explain what is taught on recognizing the power of faith:

_____

_____

_____

4. Explain what is taught on relinquishing self ownership to God:

_____

_____

_____

Challenge Complete _____ Date _____
                        (Student Signature)

Challenge Complete _____ Date _____
                        (Leader Signature)

CHALLENGE 11

Attendance Requirement

To complete this challenge, you must attend a local church **2 Sunday School classes** in your local church. The church you attend must comply with the standards that God has outlined in the Bible. He requests that we worship at a Bible-believing, Bible-teaching church that preaches salvation through grace and not by works. Baptism is taught as a sign of obedience and not a requirement for heaven. They must believe the Bible is the Word of God and is without error, preserved as such for the believer.

Church Attended _____ Date _____

Sunday School Class Attended _____ Date _____

Teacher's Signature _____

Challenge Complete _____ Date _____
(Student Signature)

Challenge Complete _____ Date _____
(Leader Signature)

CHALLENGE 12

It's Personal Daily Journal

To complete this challenge, you must complete 10 days of the *It's Personal* Daily Journal. They do not have to be 10 days in a row and you can continue in your workbook while you are logging your 10 days of daily communication with God. You also do not need to utilize all five forms of communication every day, though the more forms you use, the closer you will grow to our Lord.

Challenge Complete _____ Date _____
(Student Signature)

Challenge Complete _____ Date _____
(Leader Signature)

CHALLENGE 13

300 Club—Participation Club

To complete this challenge, you must score at least 75 points in **one** seven-day period. If you will do this four times in one month, you will earn membership in the RU 300 Club.

If you attend an RU discipleship class, please write your score on your challenge group score card and give it to your group helper so your score will be added toward earning 300 points for the month. Though this challenge only requires that you score 75 points for one week, I encourage you to earn this total every week for at least one month. If you will score 300 points per month, you will be surprised how fast you will grow spiritually.

Challenge Complete _____ Date _____
(Student Signature)

Challenge Complete _____ Date _____
(Leader Signature)

Church Service Attendance
(10 points for each)

Sunday School _____

Sunday Morning _____

Sunday Evening _____

Mid Week _____

RU Class _____

**Total points
for Attendance:** _____

300 Club

Daily Journaling
(4 points for each day)

Sunday _____

Monday _____

Tuesday _____

Wednesday _____

Thursday _____

Friday _____

Saturday _____

**Total points
for Journaling:** _____

Miscellaneous Points

Challenges completed for the week (4 points each) _____

Wearing an RU uniform and/or awards (5 points) _____

Distributing 7 RU brochures in a week (5 points), or _____

Placing a poster in a place of business (5 points), or _____

Attending a church-sponsored outreach (5 points) _____

Total Miscellaneous Points: _____

TOTAL WEEKLY POINTS

Service Total:	Journaling Total:	Miscellaneous Total:	WEEK'S TOTAL:
_____	_____	_____	_____

CHALLENGE 14

Service Opportunity

To complete this challenge, you must perform an act of peace that leads to an individual feeling safe from harm in either their spirit, mind, or body. If you think about it, you may realize that you have done so since the beginning of this study on peace. It does not have to be anything large or obvious. It just needs to be a word of encouragement or an act of submission to someone who has harmed you.

Act of peace shown to another _____

_____

_____

Challenge Complete _____ Date _____
(Student Signature)

Challenge Complete _____ Date _____
(Leader Signature)

CHALLENGE 15

The 27 New Testament Books of the Bible

Matthew   *Acts*
Mark   *Romans*
Luke   *I Corinthians*
John   *II Corinthians*

Galatians   *I Thessalonians*
Ephesians   *II Thessalonians*
Philippians   *I Timothy*
Colossians   *II Timothy*

Titus   *I John*
Philemon   *II John*
Hebrews   *III John*
James   *Jude*
I Peter   *Revelation*
II Peter

To complete this challenge, you must memorize the 27 books of the New Testament in order. This will help you in finding passages quickly and will enhance your knowledge of God's Holy Word.

Challenge Complete _____ Date _____
                          (Student Signature)

Challenge Complete _____ Date _____
                          (Leader Signature)

CHALLENGE 16

Memorize The First Four Commandments

Read Exodus 20:3-17, and then memorize the following:

1. Thou shalt have no other gods before me.
2. Thou shalt not make unto thee any graven image.
3. Thou shalt not take the name of the LORD thy God in vain.
4. Remember the sabbath day, to keep it holy.

When God established the Ten Commandments, He intended them to be the parameters in which His children would govern their lifestyles. When God's law of grace was administered by the death, burial, and resurrection of His Son Jesus Christ, the law of the commandments showed us our need for a Savior. Upon conversion, He figuratively writes the Ten Commandments on our hearts in the literal form of the Holy Spirit living within us.

This challenge will be to memorize the first four commandments. These commandments concern your relationship with God the Father.

Challenge Complete _____ Date _____
                        (Student Signature)

Challenge Complete _____ Date _____
                        (Leader Signature)

CHALLENGE 17

Memorize Proverbs 3:1-2

My son, forget not my law; but let thine heart keep my commandments: For length of days, and long life, and peace, shall they add to thee.   Proverbs 3:1-2

What two things does God ask us to do in these verses?

1. _____

2. _____

What three things does God promise in return for our efforts to abide by His Commandments?

1. _____

2. _____

3. _____

Do you believe these verses can help you yield to the fruit of the Spirit~Peace?   Yes or No   (circle one)

Special Note: The commandments given to us in the Bible cannot be fully obeyed in our own power. They can only be followed through submission to the Spirit's leading. I want the benefits listed in Proverbs 3:1-2 in my life, but they will only be afforded to someone who is allowing themselves to be led by the Lord. *Length of days* means that obedience will produce a productive life. A *long life* means just that– live in obedience to God's commands and God can and will extend your lifespan. Disobedience to God's commands inevitably brings a premature death. Walking under the influence of the Spirit brings benefits that cannot be measured in human terms.

Challenge Complete _____ Date _____
(Student Signature)

Challenge Complete _____ Date _____
(Leader Signature)

CHALLENGE 18

Reading lesson: Luke 8-17

To complete this challenge, you must read Luke 8-17. Below are spaces to list the topic of each chapter. Please fill in these blanks after you have completed each chapter.

Chapter 8 _____

Chapter 9 _____

Chapter 10 _____

Chapter 11 _____

Chapter 12 _____

Chapter 13 _____

Chapter 14 _____

Chapter 15 _____

Chapter 16 _____

Chapter 17 _____

Please describe how the above chapters can be applied in your efforts to experience the fruit of the Spirit~Peace.

_____

_____

_____

Challenge Complete _____ Date _____
                          (Student Signature)

Challenge Complete _____ Date _____
                          (Leader Signature)

CHALLENGE 19

Memorize The Last Six Commandments

Read Exodus 20:3-17, then memorize the following:

5. Honor thy father and thy mother.
6. Thou shalt not kill.
7. Thou shalt not commit adultery.
8. Thou shalt not steal.
9. Thou shalt not bear false witness.
10. Thou shalt not covet.

When God established the Ten Commandments, He intended them to be the parameters in which His children would govern their lifestyles. When God's law of grace was administered by the death, burial and resurrection of His Son Jesus Christ, the law of the commandments showed us our need for a Savior. Upon conversion, He figuratively writes the Ten Commandments on our hearts in the literal form of the Holy Spirit living within us.

This challenge will be to memorize the last six commandments. These commandments concern your relationship with others.

Challenge Complete _____ Date _____
(Student Signature)

Challenge Complete _____ Date _____
(Leader Signature)

CHALLENGE 20

Memorize Proverbs 16:7

When a man's ways please the LORD, he maketh even his enemies to be at peace with him.   Proverbs 16:7

We have memorized the Ten Commandments. We understand the way in which God wants us to live our lives—wholly dedicated to Him and to others. Now, what is the promise that God offers in the above verse to those who follow His Way?

_____

_____

Do you believe this verse can help you exhibit the fruit of the Spirit~Peace?   Yes or No   (circle one)

Challenge Complete _____ Date _____
                              (Student Signature)

Challenge Complete _____ Date _____
                              (Leader Signature)

CHALLENGE 21

Attendance Requirement

To complete this challenge, you must attend a local church **Wednesday evening** service in your community. The church you attend must comply with the standards that God has outlined in the Bible. He requests that we worship at a Bible-believing, Bible-teaching church that preaches salvation through grace and not by works. Baptism is taught as a sign of obedience and not a requirement for heaven. They must believe the Bible is the Word of God and is without error, preserved as such for the believer.

Church Attended _____ Date _____

Topic of Sermon _____

Challenge Complete _____ Date _____
         (Pastor's signature– signifying agreement with standards listed above)

Challenge Complete _____ Date _____
                      (Student Signature)

Challenge Complete _____ Date _____
                      (Leader Signature)

CHALLENGE 22

Are there a lot of people you know who are enslaved by fears of the spirit, soul, and mind? God encourages us to pray for one another. Below is a chart of blanks. Try to think of as many people as you can who are struggling with fear. Write their first names only in the blanks listed below. Ask God to help you remember as many people as possible. This week, you should pray for these people every day. It will be the beginning of a prayer list that will take your focus off of yourself and put it on the needs of others. (Don't worry; you can still pray for God to help you, too!)

_____   _____

_____   _____

_____   _____

_____   _____

Challenge Complete _____ Date _____
                                (Student Signature)

Challenge Complete _____ Date _____
                                (Leader Signature)

CHALLENGE 23

Memorize Romans 5:1

Therefore being justified by faith, we have peace with God through our Lord Jesus Christ: Romans 5:1

Special Note: Justified means "made right in God's eyes." At the time of salvation, you were "made right in God's eyes" (or, justified) through your faith in what Jesus Christ had done for you in His death, burial, and resurrection. You are now at peace with God.

To complete this challenge, please describe in your own words how your salvation has brought you peace with God.

_____

_____

_____

_____

Do you believe this verse can help you exhibit the fruit of the Spirit~Peace?   Yes or No   (circle one)

Challenge Complete _____ Date _____
                                (Student Signature)

Challenge Complete _____ Date _____
                                (Leader Signature)

CHALLENGE 24

Memorize Philippians 4:6-7

Be careful for nothing; but in every thing by prayer and supplication with thanksgiving let your requests be made known unto God.   Philippians 4:6

Challenge Complete _____ Date _____
                              (Leader Signature)

And the peace of God, which passeth all understanding, shall keep your hearts and minds through Christ Jesus.
                                        Philippians 4:7

Do you believe these verses can help you exhibit the fruit of the Spirit~Peace?   Yes or No   (circle one)

Challenge Complete _____ Date _____
                              (Student Signature)

Challenge Complete _____ Date _____
                              (Leader Signature)

Congratulations!   You have completed the second Reformers Unanimous Workbook. This study of the three fruits of love, joy, and peace are intended to help you in the process of becoming the new man or woman that God wants you to be.

You will now begin your Workbook #3—*Conformer* Workbook. It is a study in longsuffering, gentleness, and goodness. The first three fruits are intended to change the inward man or woman. The next three fruits are intended to change the outward man or woman. Praise God for your effort!

	Transforming- Love Tracking Chart	Date
1	Love definition	
2	Self-love definition	
3	Review Love vs. Self-love	
4	Memorize Matthew 22:37-40	
5	Essay Report on Matthew 5:1-12	
6	NIL Requirement- Chapter 2	
7	Attendance Requirement- 2 SS Class	
8	It's Personal Daily Journal	
9	300 Club	
10	Memorize I Corinthians 13:1-2	
11	Essay Report on Matthew 5:41-47	
12	Attendance Requirement- Sunday AM	
13	Word study on First Commandment	
14	Memorize I Corinthians 13:3-4	
15	Service Opportunity	
16	Word study on Second Commandment	
17	Verse Comparison Study	
18	Memorize I Corinthians 13:5-8a	

	Transforming- Joy Tracking Chart	Date
1	Joy definition	
2	Frustration definition	
3	Review Joy vs. Frustration	
4	Attendance- Sunday AM	
5	10/40 Window of Opportunity	
6	Memorize Psalms 51:12-13	
7	Reading Lesson: Philippians 1-4	
8	NT Books (Matthew – II Corinthians)	
9	Attendance- Sunday PM	
10	Memorize Psalm 126:5-6	
11	Reading Lesson: Luke 1-4	
12	NT Books (Galatians –II Timothy)	
13	NIL Requirement- chapter 3	
14	300 Club	
15	*It's Personal* Daily Journal	
16	Memorize Luke 15:10	
17	Essay report "Joy to the World"	
18	Memorize 3 John 1:4	
19	Bible Study on Joy	
20	Reading Lesson: I John	

	Transforming- Peace Tracking Chart	Date
1	Peace definition	
2	Worry definition	
3	Review Peace vs. Worry	
4	Attendance- Sunday PM	
5	Memorize Psalm 119:165	
6	NT Books (Titus- Revelation)	
7	Reading Lesson: Luke 1-7	
8	Essay Report "It is Well"	
9	Memorize Romans 8:6	
10	NIL Requirement- chapter 4	
11	Attendance- 2 SS Classes	
12	*It's Personal* Daily Journal	
13	300 Club	
14	Service Opportunity	
15	27 NT Books	
16	Memorize Commandments 1-4	
17	Memorize Proverbs 3:1-2	
18	Reading Lesson: Luke 8-17	
19	Memorize Commandments 5-10	
20	Memorize Proverbs 16:7	
21	Attendance- midweek service	
22	Prayer list	
23	Memorize Romans 5:1	
24	Memorize Philippians 4:6-7